Humpback Whales

Humpback Whales

A Carolrhoda Nature Watch Book

by Dianne M. MacMillan

Carolrhoda Books, Inc. / Minneapolis

To my husband, Jim, my favorite whale watching partner.

Special thanks to Ruth Radlauer for her generous help, the American Cetacean Society, and The Center for Coastal Studies.

Text copyright © 2004 by Dianne M. MacMillan

Carolrhoda Books, Inc.
A division of Lerner Publishing Group
241 First Avenue North
Minneapolis, MN 55401 U.S.A.

Website address: www.lernerbooks.com

Library of Congress Cataloging-in-Publication Data

MacMillan, Dianne M., 1943–
     Humpback whales / by Dianne M. MacMillan.
     p.   cm. — A Carolrhoda Nature Watch book.
   Includes index.
   Contents: Sea Monster?—The amazing humpback—The acrobatic whale — Feeding —Travels—Life Cycle—Singing humpbacks— Protecting humpbacks.
     ISBN: 1–57505–347–0 (lib. bdg. : alk. paper)
   1. Humpback whale—Juvenile literature. [1. Humpback whale. 2. Whales. 3. Endangered species.] I. Title. II. Series
QL737.C424M23 2004
599.5'25—dc21   2003010554

Manufactured in the United States of America
1 2 3 4 5 6 – JR – 09 08 07 06 05 04

CONTENTS

Left: *An enormous humpback whale rises up out of the water.*
Above: *People once thought these gigantic animals were sea monsters.*

SEA MONSTER?

The ocean reflects the sun and the blue of the sky. Suddenly, without warning, an enormous animal rises up and hurls its body out of the water. In midair, it twists, and it lands with a sound like a crash of thunder. Through the spray of water and foam, the huge animal slides into the ocean, arching its back in a round hump. The humpback whale has made its entrance. People once thought these whales were sea monsters. What else could have such a gigantic head and such large flippers?

Each year, thousands of people go whale watching and hope to see a humpback. This whale is famous for its acrobatic leaps, called **breaches,** and for its long-distance travels. It is also known as the singer of the ocean because it creates mysterious, beautiful melodies.

Humpbacks are warm-blooded mammals that live in water instead of on land. Like all mammals, they breathe air and bear live young that nurse, or drink milk from their mother's body. These amazing animals live in icy polar waters part of the year and warm tropical waters for the rest of the year. In spite of the outside temperatures, their huge bodies maintain a temperature of 100°F (38°C).

The sperm whale is another member of the group of animals called cetaceans.

Dolphins, smaller relatives of humpbacks, have streamlined bodies that are well adapted to living in the sea.

Humpbacks are **cetaceans** (sih-TAY-shuns). This group of animals includes whales, dolphins, and porpoises. Forty-five million years ago, the ancestors of whales lived on land. They were small, four-legged, hoofed animals similar to cows or sheep, who lived and fed near shallow waters. As time went by, they spent more time in the water. The bodies of these animals changed in certain ways to adapt, or become better suited, to living in the sea. In water, their bodies became streamlined and grew larger. Forelimbs **evolved,** or gradually changed, into flippers that helped them steer. Hind legs disappeared. Tails grew wider and evolved into two large flat lobes called **flukes.** Instead of hair or fur covering their bodies, thick layers of fat, called **blubber,** kept them warm in cold waters. To help them breathe more easily at the surface, their nostrils moved from the front of their faces to the top of their heads, where they became **blowholes.**

Above: *Toothed whales include dolphins, porpoises, and sperm whales.*
Right: *Baleen whales, such as the humpback and the blue whale, have baleen plates instead of teeth.*

Whales are divided into two groups—**odontocetes** (oh-DAHNT-uh-seets) and **mysticetes** (MIS-tuh-seets). The Greek word *odontocetes* means "sea monsters with teeth." This group of toothed whales includes sperm whales, belugas, narwhals, and beaked whales, as well as all the dolphins and porpoises. The mysticetes, or "sea monsters with mustaches," are whales with **baleen** plates that hang down from their upper jaws. They include the blue, fin, gray, sei, minke, and humpback whales.

The tubercles on a humpback's head may help the whale detect movement in the water.

THE AMAZING HUMPBACK

Humpback whales are huge. Females may reach lengths of 45 to 50 feet (14–15 m) and generally average 3 feet (1 m) longer than males. Adult males and females weigh between 30 and 50 tons (27–45 t). They average about 1 ton (0.9 t) of weight for each 1 foot (0.3 m) of length. The average humpback weighs more than eight elephants and is as long as a moving van.

Humpbacks have round bodies and massive heads. Their upper bodies are black or gray. Their undersides are usually white. The top of their heads and their lower jaws are covered with knobby bumps called **tubercles.** Each tubercle is the size of a man's fist. It has one or two stiff hairs, similar to a cat's whiskers, growing from it. The hairs are attached to a cluster of nerves that send messages to the whale's brain.

Scientists who study living things in the sea believe that the hairs help the humpback sense small movements, or vibrations, in the water. This may help them in finding food. But how these "whiskers" work and what they do is still unclear.

The whale's baleen plates, sometimes called whalebone, are made of keratin. Keratin is the same flexible material found in hair, fingernails, and the horns of cattle. A humpback may have as many as 400 dark gray baleen plates hanging from its jaw. Each plate is 25 to 30 inches (64–76 cm) long, 13 inches (33 cm) wide, and less than 0.2 inch (0.5 cm) thick. The outer side of the plate is smooth. The inner side is covered with coarse bristles, a fringe that hangs down like curtains. A humpback's open mouth looks like a huge hairy doormat. The plates and fringe wear down from use, but like our fingernails, they grow continuously throughout a humpback's life.

When baleen whales feed, they open their mouths and take in large gulps of food and water. The baleen plates strain, or filter out, the food from the water in the same way as a spaghetti strainer does.

Fringes hanging from the baleen plates strain the whale's food from the water.

Left: *A humpback's flippers can be 15 feet (4.6 m) long.*
Below: *The dorsal fin is on top of the hump that gives humpbacks their name.*

A humpback's huge flippers are one-third the size of the whale's body and measure up to 15 feet (4.6 m) long, larger than those of any other whale. Flippers help the animal steer as it swims in the water. The edges of the flippers are scalloped, or wavy.

Two-thirds of the way back from the whale's head is a small **dorsal,** or back, fin. It sits on top of a small hump. Often the dorsal fin is scarred and battered. The different patterns of scars on humpbacks' fins help identify individual whales.

Whales can be identified by the white markings on the undersides of their tails.

A humpback's tail is V-shaped. A whale's tail moves up and down as it swims, instead of side to side like that of a fish. It works like a powerful paddle, pushing the whale through the water. The tail's flukes, which may be up to 18 feet (5.5 m) across, are made of tough muscle tissue.

The undersides of the tail flukes have patches of white markings. As a humpback dives, it throws its tail upward so the white markings can be seen. The pattern of markings is different on each whale. Scientists take photographs of a whale's unique tail pattern so that they will be able to identify the animal later. Photo-identification has helped scientists learn about the travels, social behavior, and size of humpback populations.

14

One of the first whales identified by its fluke pattern was given the name Salt. She was first seen in 1970, off the coast of New England. Each spring, biologists and whale watchers eagerly await Salt's return to this feeding ground. Eight times, Salt has brought a new **calf,** or baby, with her.

A humpback's skin is less than 0.5 inch (1 cm) thick. Its smooth surface helps the whale glide through the water. The skin of a humpback's tail, throat, and flippers is often covered with **barnacles.**

Barnacles are small **crustaceans,** or hard-shelled animals, 2.4 inches (6 cm) in size. They attach themselves to a whale's skin. A barnacle does not feed on the whale it rides on. Instead, it eats **plankton,** tiny animals and plants floating in the seawater.

A humpback may be weighed down with up to 1,000 pounds (450 kg) of barnacles. But warm water makes barnacles die and fall off. This may be one of the reasons humpbacks travel to warm waters. Biologists also think that a humpback may be getting rid of barnacles when it leaps and slams its body on the surface of the water. When barnacles fall off, they leave circular scars on the whale's skin.

Barnacles often cover the skin of a whale's throat, tail, and flippers.

Some of the other round scars on a humpback's skin are caused by a small shark called a cookie cutter shark. This shark bites off and eats round chunks of whale skin. **Cyamids** also feed on whale skin. Cyamids are tiny crablike creatures less than 1 inch (2 cm) long. They are also known as whale lice. Each of their 10 legs has a hook that holds it onto the whale's skin. Cyamids do not cause serious harm to the whale.

Beneath the skin is a layer of blubber up to 6 inches (15 cm) thick. Blubber gives humpbacks their rounded shape. Without this layer of fat, whales would freeze in cold waters. The blubber keeps them warm and helps them float.

Humpbacks breathe air through a blowhole divided into two parts like your nose. A humpback has muscles that control the opening and closing of its blowhole. During a dive, thick lips keep the blowhole closed so water doesn't go in. The splash guard, a ridge of skin around the blowhole, holds water away from it when the lips are open.

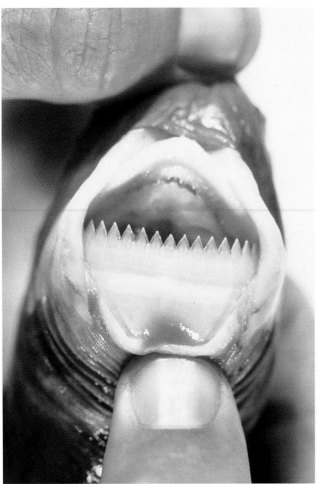

Small creatures called cyamids (top) *and cookie cutter sharks* (left) *feed on the whales' skin.*

16

As soon as a humpback surfaces, a spout of air, water, and mucus, a protective bodily fluid, shoots out of the blowhole. The mucus and warm air come from the whale's lungs. This spout, or blow, looks like a bushy tree and extends up to 10 feet (3 m) into the air.

The sound a humpback makes when it blows is a long deep "pfoouuh," followed by a brief whistling sound as the whale inhales. Humpbacks take several quick breaths every two to three minutes when they are on the surface.

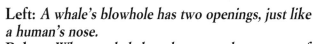

Left: *A whale's blowhole has two openings, just like a human's nose.*
Below: *When a whale breathes out, a huge spout of air, water, and mucus shoots out of its blowhole.*

Humpbacks can stay underwater for long periods of time and dive to depths that would be impossible for humans. Before a dive, a humpback takes three to seven breaths, storing the extra oxygen from the air in its blood and muscles. Then it humps its back and slides into the water. As the whale descends, it relaxes, slowing its heartbeat. This lowers the amount of oxygen that the whale's body uses. The amount of blood that flows to its flippers and flukes is reduced, but blood flow to the heart and brain increases.

Underwater, at depths of 500 to 700 feet (150–200 m), the whale's lungs slowly collapse, forcing all air out of them. This keeps the lungs from absorbing nitrogen gas from the air. (Nitrogen gas bubbles forming in the bloodstream cause human divers to become sick when they come to the surface too quickly.)

A humpback can dive 500 feet (150 m) underwater and stay under for 25 minutes or longer.

Whales sleep near the surface of the water.

Once the humpback's lungs have collapsed, the blood and muscles release stored oxygen to the heart and brain as needed. The humpback can stay underwater for at least 25 minutes. The longest recorded humpback dive was 45 minutes. After a dive, the humpback surfaces to breathe.

Humpbacks do not breathe automatically, like land animals and humans. They must think about holding their breath when they are underwater and then rise to breathe every 15 minutes or so. For this reason, whales sleep near the surface with their blowholes exposed. Researchers have learned that one side of a whale's brain sleeps while the other side remains awake.

A breaching whale will lift out of the water and land on its back. Photo was taken under National Marine Fisheries (NMFS) scientific research permit #633 issued to Hawaii Whale Research Foundation (HWRF).

THE ACROBATIC WHALE

Humpbacks are the most acrobatic of all the whales. They breach, **spy-hop, lob-tail,** and slap their flukes, flippers, and head against the surface of the water.

A breach is the most exciting movement to watch. It is also the most unexpected because it begins underwater. The whale swims toward the surface at full speed. Then, pumping its flukes, it leaps out of the water almost as high as it is long, up to 45 feet (14 m). As it falls, the whale twists and lands on its back, creating a huge splash. As it twists, it flings its flippers wide.

Humpbacks breach more often than other baleen whales. This may display strength, warn of danger, or show excitement. Humpbacks breach both when meeting other whales and when alone. Some breach as many as 40 times or more in a row. Often humpbacks begin breaching when the wind rises. No one knows why.

When lob-tailing, a whale waves its tail back and forth, then slaps it on the water's surface with a loud crash.

Because their eyes are on the sides of their heads, humpbacks have good vision above and below them and to the sides, but they can't see directly in front. They may spy-hop to get a better look. When spy-hopping, a whale lifts the front third of its body straight up out of the water. The tail flukes hold the whale in that position while it turns its head to look around.

When a humpback sticks its tail out of the water and waves it back and forth, it is lob-tailing. After several waves, the whale slaps its tail on the surface with tremendous force, producing a thunderous crash that may be heard 1 mile (1.6 km) away. Whales often slap their tails repeatedly, sometimes 50 times or more. The purpose of lob-tailing is not known, but it might be a warning to other whales. Humpbacks lob-tail more when the sea is rough and stormy.

21

Sometimes humpbacks swim on their backs with their flippers raised.

Humpbacks also slap their front flippers on the water. The whale swims near the surface, then turns on one side. It waves the top flipper, then slaps it on the water one or two times.

Sometimes a humpback lies on its side, keeping its flipper raised, for nearly 1 hour. Humpbacks also swim on their backs with both flippers in the air. As a humpback dives, surfaces, breaches, twists, turns, and swims upside down and then sideways, it seems as if it is performing an underwater ballet.

Huge humpback whales feed mainly on krill, tiny shrimplike animals.

FEEDING

Humpbacks feed in the upper parts of the ocean. These enormous whales with huge mouths eat some of the smallest food in the sea. During the summer months, a humpback whale may eat more than 4,000 pounds (1,800 kg) of plankton and **krill** a day. Krill are 10-legged crustaceans that look like tiny shrimp. Humpbacks also eat small fish, such as capelin, herring, mackerel, sand lance, and sardines.

Humpbacks belong to the family of whales called **rorquals,** or "pleated whales." These whales have 14 to 35 pleats, or folds, that run from their lower jaws to their stomachs. The pleats expand like an accordion when a whale opens its mouth. With the expanding pleats in its throat, a humpback's mouth is wide enough to hold a small car.

Above: *The whale's huge tongue forces the water out of its mouth as the baleen plates strain out the krill.*
Right: *Pleats in the humpback's throat expand when it takes in food and water.*

When it feeds, a humpback whale opens its mouth and takes in as much as 500 gallons (2,000 l.) of water and food. Then it closes its mouth. Its huge tongue, weighing close to 4,000 pounds (1,800 kg), forces the water out between the baleen plates. The krill and other food is trapped by the fringe on the plates. The whale then uses its tongue to push the trapped food down its throat.

Humpbacks have several methods of catching food. The **bubble net** is often used by Pacific Ocean humpbacks. First, a whale dives to about 50 feet (15 m) below a school of fish. Then it swims upward in a wide circle, blowing bubbles from its blowhole, making a noise like a steam engine. As the bubbles rise to the surface, the fish crowd together into a tight group in the center of the bubble circle. Then the humpback lunges into the center of the circle and devours the fish.

North Atlantic humpbacks make a **bubble cloud.** A whale releases a huge volume of bubbles all at once near a school of fish. The cloud of bubbles prevents the fish from seeing the lunging whale until it is too late.

Scientists have discovered that humpbacks change their feeding methods when catching different prey. In one instance, the bubble cloud worked with herring, but sand lance were not fooled and swam away. Whales learned to slap the water with their tails before making their bubble clouds. The tail slapping seems to stun sand lance and keep them inside the cloud where they can be easily caught.

When large amounts of food are available, humpbacks may hunt in groups of six or more whales. The group herds the fish to one spot, and then the whales take turns diving and lunging upward to eat, filling the air with shrieks, grunts, and trumpeting noises that disorient the trapped fish.

A group of whales catches food by making a bubble net.

Humpbacks do not stay in feeding groups for long. Each whale needs an enormous amount of food, and most schools of fish are too small to make a meal for more than one whale. A humpback may be alone for one feeding lunge. A few minutes later, it may be joined by other humpbacks, and they may cooperate in making a bubble net or cloud. But after a few lunges, they split up and feed alone.

When food is plentiful, humpbacks feed together in noisy groups.

Pacific humpbacks spend the summer feeding around Glacier Bay, Alaska.

TRAVELS

Humpbacks are found in all of the world's oceans. The three largest populations of humpbacks are those living in the North Pacific Ocean, those living in the North Atlantic Ocean, and those that roam the oceans of the Southern Hemisphere.

In the summer, humpbacks live in cold polar waters, where they feed. In winter, humpbacks **migrate,** or move, to warm waters, where they mate and give birth to calves. Most humpbacks go through the fall and winter months without eating. The plankton and krill the animals normally feed on are not abundant in warmer water. But the humpbacks have stored enough food in their bodies as blubber to go as long as eight months without eating.

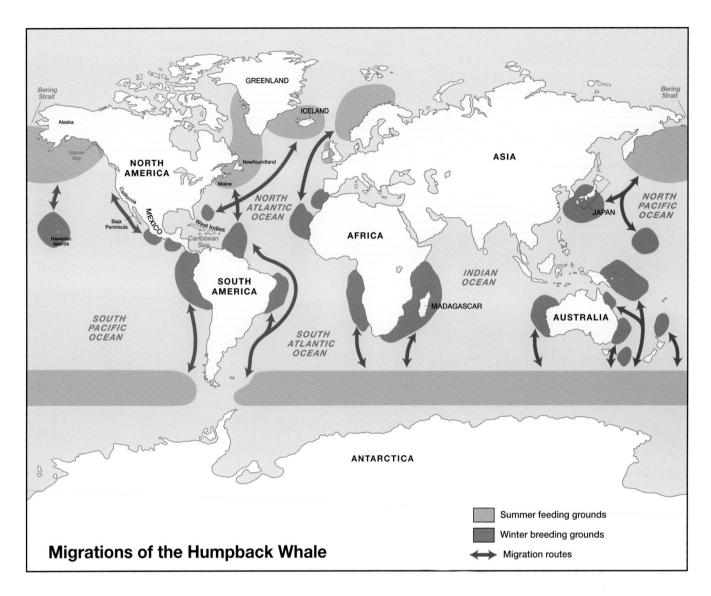

Migrations of the Humpback Whale

▨	Summer feeding grounds
▨	Winter breeding grounds
◄►	Migration routes

Humpbacks spend many months every year migrating. Some North Pacific humpbacks feed in Alaska's Bering Strait and Glacier Bay in the summer months. As the weather cools in November, they begin a long journey to the Hawaiian Islands and the islands south of Japan. Other North Pacific humpbacks spend the summer in central California and migrate to the Baja coast of Mexico.

North Atlantic humpbacks spend the summer in the Gulf of Maine, off the coast of New England, and off Newfoundland, Greenland, and Iceland. In winter, they migrate to the West Indies in the Caribbean Sea.

Some humpbacks spend summers in the waters around Antarctica.

Whales in the Southern Hemisphere feed near Antarctica in the summer months of November to May. Many spend their winters (June to October) near Australia, the islands of the South Pacific, and in Antongil Bay in Madagascar. Others migrate to the islands of the Caribbean Sea. These southern whales never meet the North Atlantic whales because the North Atlantic whales are in the Caribbean from November to May, when the Southern Hemisphere whales are near Antarctica.

Most humpbacks swim far out in the ocean during their migrations. They do not feed or sleep. Day and night, without stopping, they swim at speeds of 3 to 9 miles per hour (5–14 km/h) in large, loose groups. They communicate with one another by making clicking sounds and whistles. Humpbacks have unbelievable endurance, traveling over 1,000 miles (1,600 km) per month. Each migration takes 1 to 3 months.

How humpbacks are able to migrate thousands of miles, then find their way back to the same feeding grounds or breeding areas, is a mystery to biologists. They think calves may learn the routes from their mothers.

One researcher discovered that blue whales find their way by making very low sounds that bounce off the shoreline. Humpbacks may do the same. But some marine biologists think that humpbacks use the temperature of the water or the earth's magnetic field to find their way. Many migrating animals, such as honeybees, sea turtles, and birds, keep track of their direction by using the lines of magnetic force that extend between the earth's North and South Poles. Small particles of a form of iron called magnetite have been found in the brains of humpbacks. The magnetite, which acts like a magnet, may help humpbacks detect the magnetic pull of the earth and tell them the direction they are swimming.

Scientists have discovered that migrating blue whales make low sounds that bounce off the shoreline to help them find their way.

These scientists are attaching a radio transmitter to a humpback whale.

Most humpbacks migrate between the same locations year after year. But a few end up in different places. Biologists tag and track whales to learn their migration routes. A whale tag is about the size of a small flashlight. It contains a radio transmitter that runs on a battery. Often the scientist uses a small crossbow to shoot a tag at a whale. If the shot is successful, the tag attaches to the whale's back behind the blowhole. The tag can tell when the whale is at the surface. When the whale surfaces, the transmitter sends its location to a tracking satellite circling the earth. By tracking whales by satellite, scientists hope to better understand humpbacks' migration patterns.

When humpbacks return to warm waters, they often swim together in pods.

LIFE CYCLE

Without the need to search for food in warmer waters, humpbacks become more social. Individuals may swim with other whales. These social groups are called **pods.** Around Hawaii, most pods have 2 to 3 members, but pods with as many as 15 individuals have been sighted. In the Caribbean and West Indies, pods usually have 2 to 12 members. Whales belong to a pod for a short period of time, a few days at most. Pod members are not related. Adults tend to associate with other adults, younger whales with others their age. Young whales often spend time alone, but they become more sociable as they grow older.

Mating always takes place in the winter, when whales are in warm waters. The **cow,** or female, chooses her mate. The **bull,** or male, she chooses often swims with her for a day or two. He is called the **primary escort.**

Sometimes the chosen bull is challenged to a fight by another bull. The two fighting males swell their throats to appear larger and blow bubble trails. They use their flukes and flippers to hit one another. The males also ram their heads into each other's bodies. Sounds of their fighting can be heard for miles. Despite the size and power of the fighters, injuries are usually minor. Most of the time, the challenger gives up and the primary escort continues with the female.

Above: *A primary escort bull whale threatens a challenger with his raised flukes. Photo taken under NMFS research permit #882 issued to Hawaii Whale Research Foundation.* **Right:** *A bull humpback courts a female by blowing bubbles under her.*

After mating, the male leaves. The calf grows inside the mother for about 1 year. Calves are born the following year, when the mother returns to warm waters. A calf does not have a layer of blubber when it is born, so it might freeze in colder waters. At birth, this big baby is 12 to 16 feet (3.7–4.9 m) long and weighs nearly 2 tons (1.8 t).

The baby is probably born tail first. The mother quickly pushes the calf to the surface so it can breathe. She stays by the baby as it takes its first breaths. It's impor-tant for the calf to learn how to breathe so it doesn't drown. The baby is able to swim, but it will be a few weeks before it has enough blubber to be able to float.

Nursing a baby underwater is not easy. The mother humpback turns on her side and supports the calf with her flippers. Her nipples are enclosed in slits near her tail. Using strong muscles, she pushes her nipples through the openings and squirts a thick stream of milk into the calf's mouth. The baby nurses quickly for a few seconds and then surfaces for a

breath of air. To get enough milk, the calf will nurse 40 times each day.

The mother feeds her newborn up to 1,000 pounds (450 kg) of milk every day. That's the same as drinking 2,000 glasses of milk. Whale milk is as thick as cottage cheese. It is rich in protein and minerals and contains 40 to 50 percent fat. In contrast, cow's milk contains about 4 percent fat, and human milk contains 2 percent fat.

Calves grow quickly on the rich milk. They gain 75 to 100 pounds (34–45 kg) every single day. That's almost 4 pounds (1.8 kg) an hour. In a few weeks, the calf weighs about 6,000 pounds (2,700 kg). This rapid increase in weight helps the calf grow a layer of blubber to keep it warm and help it float.

There is a close bond between mother and calf. Sometimes the mother supports the calf on her broad back. But usually, the calf swims just to the side of the mother's head. The mother may stroke the calf with her flippers.

Calves need to grow strong because they will soon be migrating with the other whales back to polar waters. Like human babies, calves learn by playing with other calves and by imitating their parents. Calves chase and bump and touch each other with their flippers. They also like to play with seaweed and floating pieces of wood.

Humpback calves swim by their mothers' side (**left and right**). *Sometimes a young calf rests on its mother's back.*

When it is between 7 and 10 months old, a whale calf is ready to go off on its own.

The mothers and calves are among the last humpbacks to leave the breeding area. This gives the calves as much time as possible to grow strong for their long journey to colder waters. By the time the mothers and calves leave, the calves have doubled their birth length and weigh 18 tons (16 t). During the migration, each mother swims close to her calf. She watches carefully for orcas, or killer whales, and sharks that might attack her calf.

As summer arrives and the whales reach colder waters, the calf begins to eat krill and other solid food. Sometime between the ages of 7 and 10 months, the calf stops drinking its mother's milk. Some calves go off on their own soon after that. Others may swim near their mothers for a few months longer.

Whales grunt, click, and chirp to communicate with each other under water.

SINGING HUMPBACKS

Long ago, sailors on the open seas reported hearing strange sounds and mysterious songs. Legends grew about ghosts and mermaids singing in the ocean. But the singers were actually humpback whales.

In the late 1960s, scientists dropped a special microphone into the ocean near the island of Bermuda. They hoped to hear the underwater sounds that they believed humpbacks were making. The microphone captured a variety of groans, roars, squeaks, high-pitched noises, and deep bass notes. The sounds made patterns, and the patterns were repeated.

37

Present-day scientists know that both male and female humpbacks produce a variety of sounds. They grunt, click, and make chirping sounds while migrating. When eating in their summer feeding areas, they yelp, trumpet, and snort. But only the males sing songs with distinct melodies.

Bulls sing in the winter months, almost always when they are on breeding grounds. When a male is ready to sing, he stops swimming. Suspended deep below the surface, he stretches out his long flippers to help him stay still. His song may last up to 20 minutes. It can be heard more than 5 miles (8 km) away. In deep water, lower notes can be heard over hundreds of miles.

The bull surfaces for air, then returns underwater. He repeats the same song over and over, sometimes for hours at a time. One long "concert" lasted for 22 hours.

A humpback can make 20 different syllable sounds, or notes. A group of syllables makes up a phrase. The whale repeats the phrase a number of times, creating a theme. Songs usually have six themes, which are always sung in the same order. All of the bulls in an area sing the same song.

Atlantic humpbacks sing different songs from those sung by Pacific humpbacks, but all humpback songs follow the same pattern, or rules. As the weeks go by, the songs change, and all the males in the area sing the new changes. The song sung in an area at the beginning of the winter is very different from the song that is sung at winter's end.

Scientists are unsure what the songs mean. Some feel that they are mating calls used to attract passing females. Perhaps a female chooses the best singer as her mate. Others think the purpose is to warn other males to stay away.

No one knows how humpbacks produce their songs. Whales don't have vocal cords, bands of tissue in the throat that vibrate and produce sounds. Scientists believe that whales may sing by circulating air through the tubes that take air into their lungs. But no air escapes as a humpback sings, and its mouth doesn't move.

Left: *A bull humpback rests in the water with flippers outstretched as he begins his song.*

Early whale hunters went whaling in open boats like this modern one.

PROTECTING HUMPBACKS

Humpback whales have few natural enemies. Orcas and sharks attack young calves or old or sick adults during migration. But humans pose the only serious threat to a humpback's safety.

For most of recorded history, humans have hunted many different kinds of whales. Early Native American and Inuit people of Greenland and other Arctic areas killed whales that became stranded on shore or in shallow water. Humpbacks are slow swimmers and swim close to shore, so they are one of the easiest whales to kill. By the 1800s, whalers from many countries used hand-thrown harpoons, or barbed arrows, to hunt for whales.

Blubber was melted and made into soap and lamp oil. Bones were ground up to make fertilizer. Baleen was made into umbrellas, buggy whips, boot laces, and ladies' hoop skirts. Every part of the whale was used.

Left: *Whalers in the 1800s sailed around the world hunting whales in sailing ships.*
Above: *Factories on ships and on shore quickly process whales for meat and oil.*

As technology improved, whalers began to use bigger and faster ships. Instead of hand-thrown harpoons, they used guns that fired explosive harpoons. Millions of whales were killed and hauled aboard "factory ships" that could completely process all of the whale parts in less than an hour.

In the twentieth century, many people became concerned over the destruction of whales. In response to public outcry, the International Whaling Commission (IWC) was established in 1946. In 1966, the IWC passed a law that made it illegal to hunt humpbacks in any ocean. In 1972, the United States passed the Marine Mammal Protection Act. This law made it illegal to harm any marine mammal in United States waters. But hunting for whales continued in other parts of the world.

Finally, in 1986, the IWC imposed a complete ban on commercial whaling. Only two types of whaling are permitted. Native people are allowed to kill a limited number of whales for their own use. And scientists may kill a limited number for scientific study.

It is no longer necessary, however, to kill whales in order to study them. Scientists in Australia have perfected methods of taking small cell samples from a whale's bodily wastes. From these samples, the scientists can tell the animal's sex, if it is healthy or sick, and what food it has eaten. Other scientists use special crossbows or rifles to fire darts at whales to collect small bits of flesh without harming the animals. These bits can give researchers information about the sex of the animal and how they are related to other whales.

At one time, the world's humpback population numbered over 100,000 individuals. By the time laws were passed to protect whales, the number of humpbacks in the North Pacific had dwindled to fewer than 1,000 individuals. There were even fewer in the Southern Hemisphere. With the laws in place, the number of humpbacks is increasing. Scientists estimate that there are approximately 30,000 humpbacks in the world's oceans.

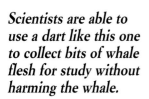

Scientists are able to use a dart like this one to collect bits of whale flesh for study without harming the whale.

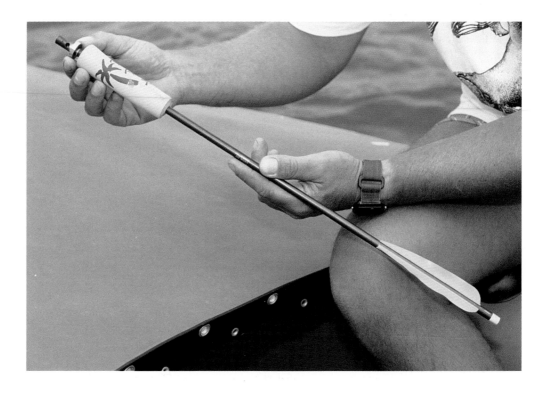

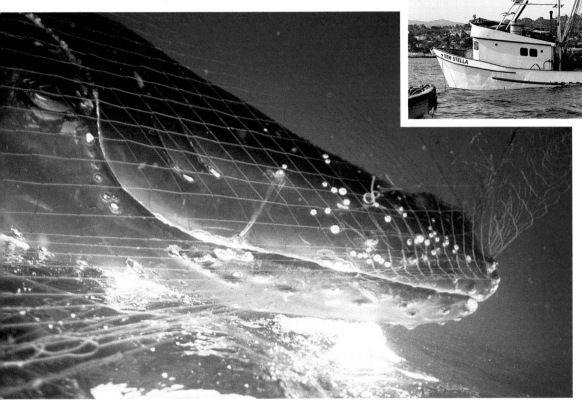

Fishing boats cast out huge nets to catch fish (right), but often whales become caught in them and drown (below).

Besides whaling, other threats to whales are the drift nets and coastal gill nets that are used to catch fish. Drift nets are huge nets made of nylon that are left to drift in the ocean for 8 hours or more. The animals that become entangled cannot free themselves, so they drown. Hundreds of thousands of whales, dolphins, seabirds, and turtles have died in drift nets. In 1993, the United Nations banned the use of drift nets larger than 2 miles (3 km) across in international waters. Gill nets are smaller than drift nets, but they also drown entangled animals.

Pollution has also become a major problem to whales and other marine life. Fish and plankton are poisoned by chemicals and garbage dumped into the ocean. When whales eat the poisoned fish and plankton, they eat the chemicals too. Harmful chemicals, such as mercury, cadmium, arsenic, and copper, collect in the whale's organs, resulting in slow death.

To save whales, we must stop killing them and we must protect the oceans they live in. The United States has set aside places of safety, called sanctuaries, to protect and study whales and other marine animals. One sanctuary includes the area surrounding the Hawaiian Islands. Another sanctuary is the Gary E. Studds/Stellwagen Bank off the coast of Massachusetts. In these safe areas, boats and people must stay a certain distance away from the whales that are visiting there.

Marine biologists still have a great deal to learn about humpbacks. Much of their lives remains a mystery. The more people study these magnificent animals, the closer they will come to solving these mysteries.

People from all nations need to work together to control whale hunting and protect humpback whales. We must save these large cetaceans so that future generations can marvel at their graceful acrobatics and listen to their beautiful songs.

Above: *Whales sometimes beach themselves when they are ill.*
Right: *A breaching humpback whale is a treat for whale watchers.*

GLOSSARY

baleen plate: a keratin fringe that hangs from a humpback's top jaw

barnacles: small, single-shelled sea animals that live on whales, the bottoms of boats, and rocks

blowholes: nostril-like openings on a whale's head through which it breathes

blubber: a layer of fat under the skin that keeps a humpback warm and helps it float

breaches: a whale's acrobatic leaps out of the water

bubble cloud: a cloud of bubbles released by a whale to confuse fish

bubble net: a circle of bubbles released by a whale under a school of fish to trap them

bull: a male whale

calf: a young whale

cetaceans: the group of animals that includes whales, dolphins, and porpoises

cow: a female whale

crustaceans: hard-shelled animals

cyamids: tiny creatures that live on whales and eat their skin, also called whale lice

dorsal: located on the back, such as a dorsal fin

evolved: developed over a very long period of time

flukes: the two lobes of a whale's tail

krill: small shrimplike animals that live in cold waters

lob-tail: a movement in which a whale sticks its tail out of the water, waves it, then slaps it on the surface

migrate: to move from one location to another

mysticetes: whales that have baleen plates rather than teeth

odontocetes: toothed whales

plankton: tiny plants and animals living in seawater

pods: groups of whales

primary escort: the male humpback with which a female chooses to mate

rorquals: whales that have expanding folds running from their lower jaws to their stomachs

spy-hop: a movement in which a whale lifts its body out of the water and looks around

tubercles: knobby bumps on a humpback whale's head

INDEX

ABOUT THE AUTHOR

Dianne M. MacMillan, a former elementary school teacher, has published both fiction and non-fiction children's books. Among her many titles are books about California history, holidays, and endangered animals. As with *Cheetahs,* also a Nature Watch Book, Ms. MacMillan hopes to encourage young readers to continue the fight for species survival. She lives with her husband in Anaheim Hills, California.

PHOTO ACKNOWLEDGMENTS

The photographs in this book appear courtesy of : © Michael S. Nolan/Seapics.com, front cover; © James D. Watt/Visuals Unlimited, p. 2; © Duncan Murrell/Seapics.com, pp. 4-5; © Masa Ushioda/Seapics.com, pp. 6, 37; © James D. Watt/Seapics.com, pp. 7, 19, 36, 38; © Brandon D. Cole/Visuals Unlimited, pp. 8, 24 (top), 25, 34; © James C. Watt/Watt Wildlife Library/Visuals Unlimited, p. 9; © Alan Desbonnet/Visuals Unlimited, p. 10 (top); © John D. Cummingham/Visuals Unlimited, pp. 10 (bottom), 12, 13 (bottom); © Amos Nachoum/Seapics.com, pp. 11, 35; © Todd Pusser/Seapics.com, pp. 13 (top), 24 (bottom); Captain Budd Christman/NOAA Photo Library, p. 14; © Robert L. Pittman/Seapics.com, p. 15; © Bob Cranston/Seapics.com, p. 16 (top); © Gwen Lowe/Seapics.com, p. 16 (bottom); © Charles Sanders/Visuals Unlimited, p. 17 (inset); © Pieter Folkens/Seapics.com, p. 17 (bottom); © Yves LeFevre/Seapics.com, p. 18; © Phillip Colla/Seapics.com, p. 20; © David B. Fleetham/Seapics.com, p. 21; © Mark Carwardine/Seapics.com, pp. 22, 41 (right); © Ingrid Visser/Seapics.com, p. 23; © Joe McDonald/Visuals Unlimited, p. 26; © Tom Walker/Visuals Unlimited, p. 27; Commander Richard Behn/NOAA Photo Library, p. 29; © Mike Johnson/Seapics.com, p. 30; © Jim Harvey/Visuals Unlimited, p. 31; © Oswaldo Vasquez/Seapics.com, p. 32; © Doug Perrine/HWRF/Seapics.com, p. 33 (top); © Drew Bradley/Seapics.com, p. 33 (bottom); © Doug Perrine/Seapics.com, pp. 40, 41 (left), 42, 45; © Daniel W. Gotshall/Visuals Unlimited, p. 43 (top right); © Brian & Cherry Alexander/Seapics.com, p. 43 (bottom); © Marilyn Kazmers/Seapics.com, p. 44.